Kite Flying

By the same author:
Knock Knock, 2007

Kite Flying

Nick Hobson

Kite Flying by Nick Hobson

Editorial Assistance: Karin Fernald

Typography and Illustrations: Andrew Evans

Typography: Richard Mason,
University of Reading Typography Department

These books are available from: nick.hobson@virgin.net

First published by Nicholas Hobson in 2015
in a limited edition of 500 copies
of which this is copy No.

Nicholas Hobson
2 Daleham Mews
London
NW3 2DB

Printed in the United Kingdom by the Colt Press.

ISBN 978-0-9934970-0-1

Contents

Poems

Poems

Angels neep harps . . .

In Heaven there ~~i~~ *will* be a job for me
I'll wake, shake like a dog, and look about.
A group will form my team – and then a shout
Enfolding me into confraternity.
Pay rates, pen-push schedules – all that is gone.
Un-bossed, Somehow, a bold goal swells and grows.
We mothered it: our Plan, and on our brows
The sweat beads shine. For all is to be done.
Each of us shapes our role, each to our bent.
Yes, markets must exist in paradise.
Angels need harps tuned and fripperies . . .
Star burnishing, galaxy management.
Some will journey down to minister well
To souls who watch daytime TV in hell.

Angels' Wings

Maybe we ought to go.
Outside it is dark
We'll put the toys in the box,
Dissemble the tower
Of bricks lest they fall,
Fold up the angel's wings,
Un-puzzle the games
Into the right containers.
White beards cluster the candles.
Who'll sweep up the detritus?
Maybe turn off the music
And tiptoe out of the front door.
It could be time to go home

* * *

Whoa Progress!
Take a step backwards
Like grandmother's footsteps.
Go home Abraham
To Ur of the Chaldees.
Pilgrim Fathers
Head back to Plymouth.
Re-board the train
At the Finland Station
Goodbye moon,
Neil, Go back to Earth.
Un-ripple, ripples
As the stone drops in the pond

* * *

Rivers dry up, cannot
Debouch their detritus
Into the ocean.
Once we were silver-tongued,
Now glottals gag us
And effing and blinding

And words get restive,
Murmur and mutter
Shelved in book prisons
On long sentences,
And surge for the exit
As starlings mass in the evening.

Artefacts from museums
Step out of their gold frames
To seek their provenance.
In brown hulks of churches
Icons burnish, and the haloes of saints.

      * * *

Says the customs officer
'Welcome to my country'
Where choice is spinning a coin.
Open your suitcase, please
What might it be, sir
Clear liquid in the bottle?
Under the toiletries
And personal linen
Are bankrolls of dollars.
Foreign imprints must
Be stamped by professors.

To see the Madonna
In the Cathedral Gallery
Baptism proof is needed.
All alien seeds
Are confiscate-able."

* * *

From the ice age they came.
Come to reforest us,
Green leafed, sap rising
Come again, Fraxinus.
And Alnus, Fagus, Castanea,
Quercus, Juglans and
Red berried Sorbus
Shade us from the winds
Which carry the seeds
And carry the virus.
Swell up our thickets
With dog rose and hazel
To this-ness and that-ness
That builds Jerusalem.

Palm trees go whence
To the Garden of Eden

Potatoes, here is your ticket home
Allumettes, mash,
Hash, Irish stew
Tuberosus Solanum
You served us well.
Go back to Mexico.

* * *

He saw the High Street
Some sunny Saturday.
And in the windows were
The world's good things –
White goods, wedding rings.
Chinese gewgaws, thingummies.
Shelves in supermarket aisles
Proclaimed "Two for One" deals.
Breeze swelled the dresses
On the racks, on marble slabs
Were crab and squid,
And aubergines in purple pyramid.
Lights winked in the Games Arcade
Burgers sizzled for the passing trade
And music played
But there was no one there.
No no, not one
No fly, no cat, no rat
No dosser with his dog and hat
Not even the Big Issue man.

       * * *

Xa neanu neeno Ka neanu
^ Xax athra Xax arra ^
Tala lmara gu Hazeakho
Popo ka Beboing Beboing
>Luhusa si si parana> cola gisanta
Gudu tsk tsk tsk Xax ga

This is a transliteration of the song of the Zaxaxyks. The ^
reflect the dental clicks and > the nasal whoops which punc-
tuate their spirit songs. Some anthropologists relate it to the
Melanesian cargo cults of the Pacific in the 1940s and '50s.
See Wikipedia Cargo Cults.

Hopadu ma safassasa
Malla Sayonara ourara sayonara
Fakola kola
^ Xax athra Xax arra ^
Alleluia Alleluia

Big winds blow . . . And rain more rain . . .
Power to the Xax . . . Spirit to the Xax.
On beaches and the holy mountain,
Hazakho, angels wings will descend upon us
with our wherewithal.
As flies buzz, and so do we,
prosper round the anteaters dung.
Goodbye to the bad times, goodbye. E
nergy to the Xax, spirit power to the Xax.
Alleluia Alleluia.

　　　　* * *

It will be alright.
Tell us a bedtime story
As to a fractious child.
Untangle the tale
Unwind the skein, find
The rings and the key
In a golden orange
Who will the princess marry?
Leave on the landing light.
Things have an ending.
But it will be alright.

Antology

Brave ant, Nansen ant, You navigate
The snowy pages of my book.

To what do you aspire?
Who is your mummy, your daddy?
Are you a rich ant, or poor?

Poetry is the book I read
And it occurs to me
Poems are like insects.

They are of all sorts
Gnats, midges – all du dus
Each finely articulated.

With itzy bitzy black legs.
They crawl down a page
Slowly getting nowhere.

Poems materialise
In books, in magazines.
Never flick them away.

Observe them closely
In a blue moon
Sometimes they fly.

Brands

She had a Prada bag to match her dress.
She – and her bag – had pride of Prada-ness.

'Gentleman' was a brand. Or it was once.
His accent spoke of nonchalance.

There nests between her breasts a silver cross.
Does she believe that Jesus died and rose?

Candlepower

I dine alone tonight. What shall I cook?
Hamburger, peas, a finger of Stilton.
And when the table's set, a glass of wine.
While I eat, maybe I'll read a book.

And though there's ambient light – a candle,
Focussing on its dark heart, its aura,
How it whiffles with each errant puff,
Its spear up high, here is my sentinel.

Now guests I have. The bud of flame attracts
Welcome and unwelcome memories.
I cannot switch a candle on or off.
Snuff it, it hurts and sheds a drop of wax.

✕

Carpe Diem

Dedicated to Andrew Watt

Trust your star. Don't knock, the door's ajar
Here's opportunity with a big O
Tomorrow we die. Now is where we are,

Poop into the party and carry your guitar
Bring a bottle, say you're a friend of Joe.
Trust your star. Don't knock, the door's ajar

A beautiful girl will be there at the bar.
Smile a 100 watt smile and say hello.
'Tomorrow we die. Now is where we are'

If she disdains you, whistle up chutzpah.
Murmur to her 'Your eyes say . . . it's green for go'
Trust your star. Don't knock, the door's ajar.

Treat Casanova as your avatar.
The fruit will tumble on the bough, though
Tomorrow we die. Now is where we are.

You've won her heart in a coup d'etat.
It's jam today and forget tomorrow.
Trust your star. Don't knock, the door's ajar.
Tomorrow we die. Now is where we are

Cape Christmas

It's over now. We have come through.
We are past the spiteful currents and the swell,
With wreckers winking at us on the shore.
We have come through, have rounded
Cape Christmas, fearsome promontory,
And spotted on the deck, on the larboard side,
Mount Santa with its cap of cloud.

And now onward to the New Year Islands
Into un-diary-ed anno domini.
What odours will they carry on the breeze?
Cannibal feasts or incense-bearing trees?

Club

May it be now, as will be, as it was:
Scottish links and Bobby Locke hangs there.
It's man-space (no flowers, a bit austere),
Writ on boards in gold the competition scores.
The steward does not wear a customer smile,
Nods 'Mr Hobson' (for I a member am).
There, by the fire the silver trophies gleam
With *Field* and antique *Punch*es in a pile.
The menu's Roast and Steak and Kidney pie,
The talks about the greens and handicaps
And match psychology, and blazered chaps
With stags (no Windsor knot) upon their tie.
And from the bar old boys can see the tee:
'That lad', they say, 'his swing is . . . poetry'.

Darling

Cannot do it. Can do
Dentistry . . . Daredevil . . . Disaster.
But not it. Yes, thespians
Patter it out. My Mum did.
'Precious' 'Duckling' 'My Sweet',
Such endearments are,well,
Like pulling teeth.

Was it me? Was it
The old school tie?
Did I react to the 'Brave New World?'
Is demonstrable love,
Like uranium, better locked up?
Love these days is on tap,
Gushes out, hot and cold.
Is the act of love now
More than a crap?

Dragons were loose

There was a time, a thousand years ago,
In the time of drugs and sex and rock and roll.
 Then was different, then. Men were kings
The weather Atlantic-bred. Nations had borders,
Law was home grown. Fields had hedges,
Windbreaks for when it blew, two shillings
Bought a pint of beer. Words were common currency
Yes, there were dragons loose and ogres.
'Where there is no vision the people perish'
No statues were inscribed, few footnotes in the books
For Enoch Powell and Jimmy Goldsmith.
'Vanity of vanities, all is vanity'

He spoke to England, freedom and for parliament,
When Empire's dregs befuddled us, spat out
In Latin tags, not tellytalk, to the working class.
'New blood would change our stock' he said
'Racism' we shouted – we slavers in the past.
In lazy, liberal big heartedness and greed
We never made the choice. A generation passed.
The Tiber did not foam. Our people changed.

He juggled careers. did Abrahamic Goldenballs,
Billionaire. Buccaneer. Lord Lucan's chum,
Diversity he fought for and spoke up for barriers
From tree virus, bee virus, e-virus, sky drones,
To halt the toxic freedoms in the levelling wind.
As gardens grow, he said, so nations need protection.
And poked sticks in the juggernaut
As the Great God Globalisation rolls.

He that observeth the wind that not sow;
and he that regardeth the clouds shall not reap.
Or were they deluded knights who tilted against
The winds that blew us to where we now are ?

Eating afternoons

Stay a while, says the picture.
Allow me to show you there past the Virgin,
serene on her loggia, the donkey is toiling
up the winding path to the hilltop town.
And is it not delightful how sly Delilah,
has her hair braided, her scissors sharp?
And through the glass door along the corridor,
I invite you into blueness and greenness
and will beguile you by geometry.
It eats afternoons, does it not, my gallery?.

Hurry, says the book
If you turn the page faster
you'll find out whodunit,
who gets the girl and the last laugh,
what is revealed to riddle-me-ree.
Jacket off, I am black and white
and read under the bedclothes
and pump up your heart rate.
Sentences flash by. I go like a train
and head for the terminus and carry
the bomb that you will detonate.

Examination

I never dreamed I would be here
In my underpants, pink, stout and bent
Standing before my torturer.
He does not care a fig for my degree.
Honours has he in Pain Management.
Up and down his eyes run free
And on my feet he focuses
On ankles tarsals tendons toes,
The toes I test how hot the water is.

Eylafjallajokull

'I am of earth. I am hot and angry.
Cannot control my movements
There is much in me and it must come out.
Little I can utter out of my orifice
But dust and ashes. I am constrained.'

'We, sky people, free to come and go
On our cat's cradle of air scheduling
Need our inflow of pink carnations.
Disdain we feel for a tinpot Icelandic god
Spraying the alphabet out of its bowels'.

This Icelandic volcano erupted in 2010 disrupting air traffic.

Have a nice day

On a Swiss Alp under the cowbells
White coats will know when I die
And calculate into my pills
So I live to the full . . . until.

'Have a nice day', say the pills,
(Sitting snug in their cradles).
'Take me once every day
And smart you will be, like me'

They're special, the doctor tells,
For us go-getters, golden oldies
Who cannot swallow bitter dregs.
Or lose our marbles.

Will they do me good? They will!
Brimful with glucosamate
Vitamin rich, with cod liver oils
So full of beans I will feel.

They will boost my body's walls
Stop pesky free radicals
Big A, Big C and bone chills:
I'll radiate health. Or else.

A day is a dice. Maybe it wills
Sunshine and wine and happy hols,
Maybe mugging in a dark street
Heart-stop, heart-break, snow spills.

He talks to plants

We see him as a comic King Canute
Who, as the courtiers snigger, told the tide
'Retreat', waved his ringed finger, and so tried
To stop the clock and the Zeitgeist to boot.
We want him thus. For Progress with a P
We fear; and the past – we cannot spit it out,
And so it sits inside our flatulent gut.
And yet this man might cure our malady.
For like cures like. And in his gardens grow
Flowers and herbs he picks, dries and distils
And re-dilutes, succusses into pills
To ease our malaise, if we dare swallow.
Things change. Towers fall. Einstein's re-born.
Trends bend. Curves and cusps can dip. And tides turn.

History's Chef

Do I not have the right
To chose from the gold-tasselled menu
Of international specialities
That the maître d'hotel proffers?
I know it's expensive
But my gold card will stretch to it.

What shall I choose? Akhenaton
Or maybe the school of Giotto –
Shakespeare and the Bible are standard. –
Or Gaudi or Handel's Messiah
(Would I could send you a post card!)
The Taj Mahal is not cheap.
But, well, it is worth it.

Yes, I know there is pain:
At the Massacre of the Innocents.
I know there is conflict
Between Guelfs and Ghibbelines,
Blues and Greens, Saladin and Crusaders,
Top Hats and the Workers.
Pain as the lobster shies from the pot!.
But what a chef is history
Who, under soft lighting, lifts the lid
On the rich dishes he concocts for me.

Last night's dishes

Mop up your night sweat, your preposterous dreaming.
Descend in pyjamas into the dark kitchen
With its ho-hum electrics – and edge for the fridge.

Open the door: equable light bathes its interior.
Reason abodes. No sourness. Nothing decays there.
Your ears are not tuned to its planetary music.

Fridge is for the chosen. There is no democracy.
Butter is above bacon, eggs snug in the egg rack
A place compartmented for apricot yogurt.

In its door shelf stand tall as sentinels: milk,
Orange juice, and a bottle of Riesling.
Aspire up to its cool hierarchy:

A jelly on a plate is purple and fluted,
And as if in canopic jars, selected sauces;
And in the crisper a lettuce and a melon.

There are much goings out, much comings in
As in Heaven, as told by Hildegard of Bingen
And Dante would sing it in terzarima.

As the kitchen clock shrieks the appalling time,
You find life's detritus and last night's dishes.
Here is your haven – chilled water in a brown jug.

Let them be dangerous

Not immured at the back of the bookshop
Between the Prophet Gibril and Poems for Lovers,

Not the poor things in the poetry mags
Pleading O-eyed to be read by strangers,

Rather read by virgins under the bedclothes
Whose breasts are undreamed of,

Read by plotters as the candle gutters
As they write the manifesto,

Intoned to the wedding guests by the boozy uncle
Shocking the in-laws,

Graffiti-ed on the concrete wall
Between the razor wire and the visored police line,

Or abandoned one night. A bundle
Left at the door of the orphanage.

Someone will find them,
Someone will take them home
Coax them, nurse them
Spell out their syllables.

They will grow up as dangerous as Moses.

Lighting up

Upon a hill at dusk I saw a man:
A match flared, a flint face cupped in the glow,
His eyes bright with the buzz of nicotine
As Birmingham was lighting up below.

Once from Africa came woman and man.
Could light a sulky fire but little else.
What drugged dreams drove our forebears then
To walk and people the Americas?

Methuselah

Genesis says he lived a thousand years.
Why not me? My bowels perform.
My urine stream is strong. Doctors
And geneticists these days know how
(And yes I'd pay) to prolong life.
I like yogurt. Nor would I demand virgins.
Already have seen wars and booms and busts
Have seen a hurdy-gurdy of zeitgeists.
Maybe the saplings in the forest will
Resent the towering oak that shades their sky
Yet think how the drip-drip of wisdom
Would accrete to a golden honeycomb
And Statesmen would queue up to access me.

MYOB

I'd have you keep your snout
Our of my patch. No man's an island, but.

DNA CCTV the Net
They're after you that angry alphabet

I have a PHD. Maybe I have a soul.
I'm not a goldfish in a bowl.

Puss watches you with velvet paw.
You have no right by EC law.

I'll go stick insect –metamorphose,
Find multiple identities.

You think you're free. No one is dumber.
They have your PIN and your lucky number

X

Mystery

It's happening more these days
I'm not clear how very ordinary people
with dates with the chiropodist
and PC meetings and cleaning to collect
suddenly cease to exist.
Abduction is unlikely.

One day they're there, the next, pouf –
gone like a soap bubble
with its own bright world
but leaving a distinctive whiff.
Despite clonking great funerals
with men in top hats
to obfuscate the mystery

Unwilling to click on delete,
You wonder. Half wonder.
Out of a half-read book
Drops a postcard from somewhere in Crete
Saying 'having a lovely time. Lunch soon?'

Name them

Name them each one. Spell out each syllable.
Summon them up from the deep waters.

Dave did the layouts. Sue conjuring tricks.
Bernard and his Kawasaki.
Three Kings Richard. Don and the dogs.

Name them. Name each one.
May they not slide back into the water
Into forgotten-ness.

Sandra was old. Remember her.
Nigel had cancer. Cancer, Ann.
And Desmond, the accountant.

Are they not ours? Of our generation?
How odd they all were.
Link us too into the chain of remembering.

Name them. Name each one.
Granpa won medals. Aunty I,
She gave us the sugar bowl
Reeve even them in.

Heave all of us. Dig in
On hobnail heels to win purchase
To draw them from the dark water.

It's November and squalls gusting.
Worse is the forecast.
Let them come in, close to the fire.

No Traitor Birds

I will not tell you the coordinates
So no one finds the place to which I go.
It has three walls, no door, is open to the sky
Where a rowan gives a little shade
(A chopper could not spot me under it).
No traitor birds will tell you where I am.

My larder on a ledge holds water bottles
Slabs of chocolate, raisins in a jar.
To see beyond, some rusty rungs I climb:
Nothing much but goats, and the old rail sleepers
And in the evening a far city's glimmering.

Peace drops slowly there, and time I have
To watch the ants among the broken stones,
The drones, the myrmidons, the queen,
How they know where they go, and lug
Such heavy burdens for their colony.
I tell my stories that warriors
Build dynasties, betrayed by courtesans.

Come morning, I head home
Walking, un-purposefully, head down,
And change my coat and scarf
To adjoin the road from where I came.

Party

Let me invite you, please, to our party.
You'll meet us the now people, we in today land.
Are we not beautiful . . . doers and shakers,
Happening-makers?
Note how we dart and weave
like the fish in a coral atoll.
Feel free to circulate. Meet Lee. He paints.
Is up for the Turner. I'll fizz you up . . .
Mel in the sari is a writer for Channel 4 . . .
Dynamite stuff
Note the global throb about Rob.
He's a rock conductor.
His friend is with Charlie. Watch for the lightning
Feel the crackle of creativity. Is that the doorbell?
It must be Tati. Tati's a dancer.
She's the Versace family.
Who's that still knocking? Let them in...
let them in.

A man in a mac comes out of the weather.
Who can imagine a demeanour droller?
Maybe he's drunk though his breath is fouler.
This eye-rolling truth-telling Savonarola
Tells us that maybe the party is over.

Peephole

You, Adam, I see you.
You, Eve, I see you:

Glass is your skin, flesh is as cladding.
Into each ribcage I can see

Organs entwined like ripe fruit:
Each nudging the other, nestled together.

You are my chef d'oeuvre. You delight me.
My music is your organs in concert.

Chug on heart and lungs: oxygen steamboats
To the body's peripherals.

Pancreas, exude your juices. Perform, liver,
Glycogen-maker, maker of protein.

I name the hairs on the nape of your neck:
Nor pink sphincter's a secret.

You have done well,Captain Head:
Well done, Corporal Heart: well done, the Privates.

Sun and moon you will never see:
Work well, you dark engineers.

My peephole into your head
Brings me much laughter.

I joy in your turbulent neurons,
Uprising like a flock of starlings.

Yet evil lurks in the medulla,
As androgens skip in the corridors.

Many the models I made were:
The wolf and the owl and the dragonfly.

Stay away, leopard, glass shards, flick knives:
No fire tongues, no banging of drums.

I made you. Sacred your bodies.
Woe who rips open this parcel.

Piero and the Angel

Piero Della Francesco's Archangel Michael in the National Gallery

Archangels are God's executives.
He's done the job, has just dispatched
Satan, whose slimy head he holds.
A do-er he … you would not mess with him.

He stands, square on, well-winged, well-clad,
His skin-tight vest is air-force blue,
Pernickety his sleeves, his boots are red.
A flying saucer sits upon his head.

Why do I like it so? Let me unpick
The threads this picture weaves for me.

Well yes, good wins over evil alright.
It's good to see goodness is doing things.

Among his forbears was Masaccio.
Was Leonardo influenced by him?

Did he paint it before or after
Constantinople fell to the Turks?

From Perseus through to Superman,
Caped champions can always turn us on

The tempera painting was a triptych once
Who cut it up? What did they pay for it?

And Michael's face reminds me of a boy
Who was in the Eleven at my school.

I drank a glass or two of Orvieto
In Piero's hill-top town ten years ago.

Assignations I recall I've made
In that alcove of the Sainsbury wing.

Real art is like a Banyan Tree.
Its cabled roots accrete and multiply

Under its shade the cattle congregate
And the birds chirrup in its foliage.

A shrine it is, and from its low-hung branches
Locals suspend their votive offerings.

Pizzicato

What will it be tonight
Burger or texmex?
Thai fingerlickin vindaloo dim sum
Frog legs fish'n'chips pub grub paella?
The wheel spins, it is the happy hour
And *rien ne va plus* it is pizza pizza!

       * * *

Pomodoro Pepperoni
Andiamo anchovize
With jeepers capers oregano
And stoned or unstoned olives bedded
Deep in gungy mozzarella
Con prosciutto con salami
Chicken chaps we'll never be
Pizza's for a real fella
Fun guys, let us paint the town
Find what washes pizza down.

       * * *

Nessun dorma we will overcome
Why are we waiting us against them

Hang upon the TV screen
As fruit flies on a nectarine.

And when we score and when we score
Whole streets will hear the butane roar

Long before the final whistle
Guiseppe's oven spits and sizzles

Guts are like an open goal
Pizza pizza fills the hole

Romano con prosciutto
Con salami Napoli

Margarita Marinara
Beauties you can get your teeth in
* * *
Vespa and Honda are busy tonight
Duck and dive to segment the post codes,
The undulant crust of flat earth London.
Ding dong what's at the door?
The helmeted pizzador carries his cargo
To go with the six-packs and fruity Merlot.

Playing Possum

I know they are there.
They know I am here.
I the hunter, they the hunted
There in their lairs
In the glimmering.
Do they not know I am dead-eye dick?
My blunderbuss is cocked.
They will be curtains.

Once I could whistle up words
Once they sat on my hand.
Now they go walkabout.
I will taxiderm them
And put them in a poem.

Potter's Asthma Remedy

'Wheezy with Auntie's Abdullah?
And why so pale and loitering
With the ruddy kids in the garden?
Why so chesty this fine day when
It's cherry time and the grass is mown?
Sip Orange-aid and an Ephedrine.
Play a bit of cricket . . . join in . . . '

No, upstairs to my bedroom I go,
I want to be dark and alone
And nurse out my only relief
On a saucer in a tumulus,
Tip up the brown herby stuff
Strike a match, wait till it sputters,
As the sweet smoke builds in a puff
Inhale as the lung walls fall
Inhale as the hard sins melt
And the tears roll, roll.

Rain

Means No Games today. It's fine for me.
I'll read my book, and, if it pelts,
I test my new raincoat's belt
And demonstrate the permeability
Of boots as bubbles burst in puddles.
Means together under one black umbrella
God makes things for us well-er.

Richard Dawkins, thanks.

Undeluded us, let us look back
To fifty years ago when with one hefty swat
He dealt with religion's buzzy gnat!
You see our recent ancestors were stuck
With some hotchpotch of metaphysics
That, as it were, had misted up their specs.
Now we see clearly. We can face facts.
How sane our world has now become
When Science has its calm imperium.
What a no-godsend to say goodbye
To guilt, so we can couple soberly.
And still our spirits do a little dance
To see a Green Fossil on an ambulance.
On festivals at a village heritage site
Biddies enact quaint ceremonies
Dispensing to us wine and a biscuit
As the choirs sing evo-torios.
And come Saturday altruistic atheists
Sit by the beds of orphanages
And tell again the tales of Darwin's finches.

Death is just earth. Our peace is deep.
No longer dreams disturb our sleep.

ᕗ

Salt and Pepper

By candlelight they had calamari
And moussaka and a bombe surprise.
She told him about the baby.

* * *

They ate three rosettes: langoustines
With a tincture of anise, then rack of lamb.
They planned the merger.

* * *

They caught brown trout from the burn
Lit a fire, picked blueberries.
They had dreamed of Africa.
That night Africa dawned.

* * *

Kate and Sidney they had,
Then fried Christmas Pudding.
They sang the old songs.

* * *

People are coming to supper.
Let's set the table, flowers and a candle.
What wine? What for the main course?
After polite gallimaufering
What will we talk about? Stories:
Of what we did, what we will do.
For they are the salt and pepper
They are the supper's sauce.
Tell them again, old and new.
They are liaison for our togethering.

Sardines

This can, not from the top shelf,
Nor haute cuisine, yet speaks for itself;
Is fine for a snack or if you're more-ish,
And for one makes a nutritious dish.

Pull the ring pull – it will reveal
Three neat fat fish sit snug in oil,
Backbones in, head and tail-free,
And silver rich in Omega Three.

If alarms ring and shops are shut
And you can't go out in the street
And if your larder's under key,
What precious specie will sardines be!

Send it

It is the concatenation
of random ifs
and whens and hows
that lets a new world be
and sets it in order.

And so, absent-mindedly
this moment got born.
It was, I think, the ant
that ignited the big bang.
In triumph it ascended
my right shoulder.
The drone of the planes,
Stopped, and dust motes
made merry in the late sun,
and from the jasmine
the signals were benign.

O this moment. Save it. Send it.

Siege

If work is to be done,
– that lowering and obstinate town
That blocks the route south –
Maybe your strategy ought
Not to be pure onslaught.

Circumamubulate it
Sniff with disdain, cock a snook,
And back away like the Greek fleet
Then by night, by fire, by sword
Steal in and get in to work.

Sunday

PASSER-BY

Ding Ding Ding Ding Ding
It's Sunday and people are going to church.
Not many, old ones, biddies,
Old chaps in pee-stained suits,
A mum smarming up to the vicar.
I resent them and their allelujahs.
Sunday should be wilderness.
How dare they colonise it.!
How dare they scatter up imprecations
Like broadcasting crusts for the ducks.
They are in there with the ghost god.
They are the remnant.

CHURCH-GOER

It says in Genesis Eighteen
That Abraham bargained with God
To not smite Sodom for ten good men.
So do not we, as it were, wise virgins
Hold back clock hands against the End Time
That is undoubtedly coming?
Maybe we, unsure about Heaven,
We are the seed corn, and we the remnant
That Paul talked about in Romans Eleven.

Swiss Army Knife

I have it in my pocket safe
My clunky man, my talisman
My own Swiss Army knife

People are pain, people are grief.
Scissors will cut me free
Tucked in my Swiss Army knife

His ego balloons beyond belief.
I have a spike to puncture it
In my Swiss Army knife

From chit chat keep me aloof
A sarcastic slash and jab can do it
With a blade in my Swiss Army knife

Mealtimes no! Eat on the hoof
Have bangers and beans from the can
With tools in my Swiss Army knife

Thank You Letter

Thank you for the lovely vase.
It reminds me of you.
My eye rests on the milky glaze
And you float through.

Memories batten on
A picture, a scarf, a cup,
A book, a snatch of tune,
An oak, a peach, a corner shop.

Objects talk when I am near.
If only the past stayed stumm.
Could I then see things clear
As the un-mossed stone in the stream?

Send me your gift (though hard to post),
No ribbons or expense,
Clear of the past's crust
Send me Four Elements.

Pure they are and free to play.
They are 'is' and not 'ought',
They breathe, burn, bury, wash away
With no handcuffs for the heart.

The Cracks

Everyday people at golf clubs and business do's,
Nice normal people, no paragons indeed,
Can they really be the rivulets that feed
The skewed things we glaze over in the news?.
True, here our politicians aren't much use.
But evil's abroad all right. Where does it breed?
How can we stop it finding its way in?
Cross fingers or keep them tight in your mits
Don't pick at threads less the fabric un-knits.
Disinfect against original sin.
Children play safe, in case a bear attacks,
To step on the pave, not tread on the cracks.

The Gender Dance

Shall we dance, it is playing our tune?
Dare we step the intricate steps
Fiddledy foot-fumbling steps
Women and men did forever?

Mind mien bones body heart hair,
You are unknown. I want not what I know.
You could un-puzzle me
And I could be whole.

The God Brand

God is big. Bigger than Bill Gates
Could be Jewish. After the big bang
He got the whole shebang for a song
Went into space and tectonic plates
Diversified into bio and then went
Into massive brand development.

You never see him, him the CEO
Invisibility is part of his technique,
Though many claim they hear him speak.
(He was once painted by Michelangelo!)
Confidence is key. Without trust
He's finished and The Bank is bust.

He earns much from a spin-off niche.
The Disney Corporation can't compare
With fantasies he spirits from thin air;
Some sells in Sothebys but much is kitsch.
They generate much profit flow.
And massively enhance the God Brand.

He has risen but the price is not high sky.
In meltdown God's a speculative Buy

The Little Ones

Hear the artillery. A battle is raging.
Poor the little ones out in the forest,
Their footsteps falter on the dark path
As cold eyes weigh them and size them.
Pray they say no to the sweets proffered,
And the woodsman's cottage does not inveigle them
Don't they have a Granny these orphans?
Pure and Dear are their names, and True.

Propaganda. More proper ganda.
Poor the little ones in the city.
Wink Wink say the multiples in the High Street
As they watch TV in the plate glass window
And stop their ears to the effing and blinding
As they tuck in their cots in the red light district
Maybe the vicar will offer them salvation.
Hope and Home are their names, and Good.

Gunships above. Boys with Kalashnikovs.
Poor the little ones at the border.
Is there a place for them over the mountains?
Pity they do not have the right papers.
Cannot swim the ocean of syllables,
Cannot traverse a desert of acronyms.
Cold and hungry are the little ones.
Love and Life were their names, and Trust.

The Match

Dedicated to James D'Albiac with whom I play golf

1

Look at him swank his way out of the Pro's Shop!
'What are we playing for?' He said on the tee
'Why not a wager for the lovely Miranda?
Matchplay it is and may the best man win.
To the victor the spoils and shapely the trophy.'

2

Seven his handicap, mine was eleven,
And my gullet rose to see his demeanour
From his checkered cap to his blazoned sweater
From his studded glove to his tasselled Footjoys
And the coldness that spoke from his lidded eyes.

3

Squat on the tee there sat his equipment
Paraded out like May Day weaponry,
To be saluted by Stalinist generals.
He unhooded his driver, and awful his Cobra
(Even his putter bespoke of menace).

4

He drove off first and his swing was easy.
(A four par dogleg with pines encroaching).
He judged the angle and his ball sat pretty
Smug on the fairway, with a pitch to the green.
First tee nerves had jangled my tempo . . .

5

. . . I dollied to the right and plopped in the heather.
His four was textbook; I scrambled a bogey.
'First blood to me' was his only comment.
The second and third reached into a valley
And I clawed back a hole with a stroke to thank.

6

Look as your drive smacks into the distance,
And marvel at the course on that May morning.
Green-gowned the trees like guests at a wedding,
Prinked and expectant before the bride's entry.
So balmy it was you could take off your jersey!

7

The par three fifth is under two hundred,
If you'll carry the bunkers that shield the green
It calls for a long iron over the water.
Sweetly we feathered them as they bit on the apron,
And we heard the applause from the frogs in the pond.

8

Dew was drying and the greens were glassy
With undulant ripples disguising the borrows.
I babied mine; his snaked to the pin
And a big black bird which was perched on the rowan
Cast a beady eye on the two contestants.

9

Who is the god of golf? It must be the Colonel,
Flat-capped, plus-four'd, his mashie niblick
Under his arm, as his staff of office,
To him we pray, as our well-struck pitch shot
Over-arches the bunker to hit the down slope.

10

Oblations I offered on the daunting ninth
For two down I was . . . he drove with a swagger
Hooked, hooked to the gorse, the golden gorse.
I trusted my swing and powered my Callaway
To the grassy plateau over the gulley.

11

Did he cheat on his second? Did he nudge
His ball a bit to open up a window?
We halved it in four and in my heart I wondered
And that big black bird that seemed his familiar
Flapped away and its caw was eloquent.

12

By the Fourteenth he was one hole up.
Yet in the psyche of every match player
Dwell Yips, Fludge and Shank, three grinning demons.
And the Fata Morgana of the Perfect Swing
Lured me away to the woods and water.

13

Imagination, or-too-much-of-it, is woe to a golfer.
And we urge ourselves on, as so a jockey
Sweet-talks and curses his mount in the National.
'Keep calm' I said and I said 'Swing Easy'
As I shafted my eight iron onto the green's heart.

14

And there I saw her on the parallel fairway
The delightful Miranda – her body in action As she
swung, unleashing its parabola

As natural and carefree as a phrase of Mozart.
She waved to us both and to me she smiled.

15

Can you picture her – her whom I love –
A furnace her hair that fair May morning,
Violet-eyed and freckled like a bird's egg.
To whom I pleaded today in the Club House
To be my partner me in the Club Mixed Foursomes.

16

Green is the fairway hatched by the mower
Green are the greens which the sprinkler waters
Green too is jealousy and that was the moment
That I knew the match had turned on a sixpence:
To us she waved. To me she smiled.

17

Par three. One down. Two holes to go.
He was on the green and short was my six iron.
Sweet then to see how my chip from the apron
Leapt like a salmon as it hit the pin
And gurgled in for unbeatable birdie.

18

'Jammy' he said as he gritted his teeth.
As we came down the eighteenth even-steven,
I knew I would crush him on the final hole
He shook my hand as we walked to the Club House.
(For chivalry's sprit has fled to the golf course.)

19

Over a drink she said yes, did Miranda,
But warned me of the lament of the Golf Widow.
'Sad are the Sundays that she faces
As he swings a club and his heart paces
For the call of the course and its green embraces'.

The Willendorf Venus

Out of the limestone doll-like she came
No Botticelli she, the Willendorf Venus,
Flint-chipped, hair plaited, ochre tinted
Her hips belly boobs and pronounced vulva
Spake of fertility to queen us
In a world men-empty when aurochs abounded.

As nations need soldiers, so rose the clamor
For kinder kucher kirk and motherhood.
Dolls got cuter and if you pick her up
She'll wee, open blue eyes and say 'mamma'.
Much was the merry gemutlichkeit mood
As the dolls quaked and the guns roared.

Did from Ibsen's play pop out this chrysalis?
Barbie was born lithe, leggy, with less boob,
The doll you want to dress. For this Ms,
Who'll buy a chap a beer (and share his job),
Uni, she desired along with the guys,
Wanderlust – and one point five babies.

What seismic tremors hit our yesterdays!
The Birth Pill was high on the Richter scale
Man's tall tower tottered and the birth rate fell.
Later a thousand years later old men will prise
A living doll with bright unhuman eyes
Who coyly winks at them in the rubble.

Thin Skin

I scratch therefore I am. As Aries born
My mittened fists would box the allergies.
At ten was red and raw – and hard to prise
My gummy legs from socks that I had on
And better to be taunted by the 'leper' cries
Than hateful pity from averted eyes.
Sad that my football boots were never worn!
Those times, you see, pre-hydrocortisone.
As King of skin, each itch will get hard shrift
That dares fly its red flag in my domain,
And pleasure gets its punishment again.
But for thin skins the compensating gift
Is sensing how moods change and worlds shift
And feel the jangling of another's pain.

Today's the Day

One day we shall get up before the dawn*
And wide awake know today is the day.
What to do is: make your place spic and span.
If you have family silver, buff it to a gleam
– Candlesticks, trophies, baptismal mugs.
Put on a table the photos of your loved ones
And cover them with a dark cloth.
Pay bills and feed the cat for the day.
If the phone rings that morning, hang up.
Line up your spare keys like dead mice
Don't look in mirrors – and go to the toilet.
You are not to lock the front door.

W. B. Yeats 'Hound Voice'.

Turbulence

I believe in God, not she. We make the bed
We share. She's just as good and nice as me
And acts to cats and neighbours charitably.
Bible aside, she's read the books I've read.
If our plane crashes, what happens then?
Will she be pronged to hell, l carried away
By rescue angels? In my DNA
Is the God-gene? Or is God just my yen?
Our plane, our planet is in turbulence
We're all strapped in and going god knows where.
The steward's trolley will not reappear,
Do I imagine that the crew looks tense?
Saved or damned, let's pray we have brave souls
To captain us safe in at the controls.

USP

What is our edge? Where our go-faster-stripes
Where the bells and the whistles? We know
Little Me-Too with her pretty blue eyes
Won't survive in a Do-or-Die market.
Evolve we must – and we do not have aeons –
A rhino horn, or outrageous plumage
A wicked new beak, an add-on fragrance...
So at the Marketing Department Think Tank,
Amid the burble of the New Product
Launch Up bubbles one mantra: Where is our USP?

2

The U is for Unique. Un-better-able,
An offer you cannot refuse.

The S is for Selling. To say Yes
It will cost you. But, yes, it is worth it.

The Proposition is P, and it is to you
A rational guy, a discrete individual.

'Cleans your breath while it cleans your teeth.'
'A Mars a day helps you work rest and play.'
'Helps build strong bodies twelve ways.'
'Prolongs Active Life'

USPs do things for you. But subtle
They're not; they din things in

(A Crucifix may come handy
To ward off the vampires, Video Vampires
Who suck the blood of the message.
Distract you with extraneous graphics)

3

It was Rosser Reeves who bestrode
Madison Avenue back in the Fifties,
CEO of the Ted Bates Agency.
He was the progenitor of the USP.
I shook his hand once – felt the dark power
Glinting from his spectacles.
He came from somewhere down South,
And his Dad was a preacher.

4

Those were the days before Doyle Dane Bernbach
A pre-Saatchi era when words were primary.
Where the emperors were iconoclasts.

Now in the era of the global brand.
Advertisements cosy up to you
Tickle your fancy, target your life style
Beguile you on to their team, shy away
From the hard claims regulators pounce on

5

You are unique, no 'me-too' you.
He has made you designedly
Your ingredients are new,
You are his brand, his USP.

Strange the media that He uses
But will get His message through.
Sorrow, sickness, dreams He chooses,
For Saul and Samuel, and for you.

He has a job for you to do –
Build a bridge, nurture a fractious tot,
Overcome a demon or two,
Sing songs... Heaven only know what.

What will it cost if I believe?
Not much, for I am sure to die.
What benefit do I receive?
Why, a slice of heavenly pie!

Wicked

Wicked I was. I burn in hell.
Speak out my name. Say it without hate.
Each syllable that you enunciate
Is water to quench my fire a while.

Words Words Words

It is as if
when the traveller, his boots pinching,
fears ahead that the track is stony
and deviates a while to a grassy knoll,
wiggles his toes in the little stream,
unships his haversack, fills his flask,
then sees through the trees that the route home
winds downhill through delightful parts.

ZEUGMA

Now on comes spangly Zeugma,
who, legs akimbo, rides on the backs
of two galloping horses.
Drums rolls and she cracks her whip
and the crowds gasp to see
her jutting bosom and her horsemanship.

HYPERBOLE

Up it whooshes… then the oohs and aahs.
But look for a mo-
ment how its falling stars
illumine things below.

LITOTES

He knelt and squinted through Heaven's back
door 'What is it like?' She said.
Face radiant, he replied:
'Well, on the whole, not half bad.'

ANAGNORISIS

Did not the scarfed figure in the rear pews
Cause you to ponder? Couldn't you guess
from the Granny's whispers and the locked bureau's
clues, that Time is unwrapping amazing surprises?
The penny drops. Anagnorisis.

METAPHOR

. . . casts everyday words into a play,
and to dazzle us, switches on spotlights
to make your meaning clear as day.

IRONY 1

Because we know it is a pig of a world,
a stupid malodorous brute,
we, of course, say it is not.

IRONY 2

Fork-tongued, he is, shifty and lah di dah
And never tell things as they are

HENDIADYS

What enemy flagship can withstand the
Wham and Bang of two weighty balls
linked by the chain-shot AND?

SYNECDOCHE 1

At the Big Bang the Word
flew into a million black birds.
One flapped its ponderous wings
and after aeons learnt to fly
and roosted deep inside the dictionary.

SYNECDOCHE 2

With slippery synecdoche
Meanings get wobbly
As Part and Whole is the same
(And Champagne is Bubbly).
Hard to see elbow and arse
For the snake in the grass!

OXYMORON

That spot on my nose
was the most exasperating pimple;
To scratch it though
was pleasure and pain
pure and simple.
(But oxymoronic to do so
before my wedding photo.)

HOMONYMS

Cymbals: I clash and crash to frenzied cheers
Symbols. I'm for the inner eye, You are for ears
Cymbals: Orchestras and Jazz need our pzazz
Symbols: I metaphysical. You are tinkling brass.
Cymbals Percussion can make the foot thump
Symbols: In the dark heart we light the lamp.

HENCEFORTH

You are squeaky clean; ungoogleable;
The passport is virgin; credit rating 'A;'
In your wallet no photos of loved ones
And a thousand crisp fivers.

The suitcase is packed; so are your sandwiches.
Henceforth it shall be.

THUS

This word has a splintering impetus
So ram your logic with the thud of 'Thus . . .'

WOULD SHOULD WOULD

Could dipped a shy toe in the sea
of glassy possibility.
Should wagged a finger, invoked the law,
made the case against and for.
Would wept and sighed and wished it so.
'If only' came the well's echo.
Will did it. Hence
all are fast-forwarded into the present tense.

'TWAS EVER THUS'.

Ducks on the Village Green will wonder
If our pond is greener,
And serener in a pond-er yonder.
Drakes will quack back 'The ultimate is – us.
Things do not change. 'Twas ever thus.'

WYSIWYG

Of him beware: this fellow
who with honest eyes
peeps through the bars
wants to be taken home.

Its snout is pat-able
but crawls with sub-agendas.
Clever old evolution – it knows
What sweet meat is simplicity.

Beware the pungent urine it projects.
Everything living has a secret:
A shame or un-shout-out-able joy.

What You See Is What You Get

Some notes about my poems

- A poet needs readers. A proportion of people like verse and read it in private and internalise it and tell others because it means something to them. (Maybe more people write poems rather than reading new slim volumes). A good poem has a ripple effect and people talk about it.
- In our culture it is difficult to find a 'voice' to represent our generation or our atomised society. Poets needs a ripple effect, a focus, a critical enthusiasm and word-of-mouth momentum. The impact of their verse proves a ripple effect on the cultural pond as the Romantic movement and the French Revolution or World War 1.
- There is another thing that readers (like me) believe, that there are other ingredients in the poetry package that they are expecting. Today poets think rhyme or half rhyme as an extraneous lollipop and not for grown ups. Rhyme can deepen the intensity of the verse reflects and resonates to a parallel reality that is in the potential of language. The reader is rewarded by the poet who can understand and accept a wider continuity of English poetry.
- Should each line start with a capital letter? Verse should be different and apart from prose. Some think it's a bit fuddy-duddy like wearing

waistcoats to capitalise each verse. I think it supports the look and typographical tidiness of the poem on the page. A line of poetry has to distil and compress the content of what it seeks to say and provides a discrete morsel for the reader to swallow. Too much enjambment risks turning the content into prosey sludge.

- Bible reading a hundred years ago was the ground-bed of poetry reading which is one of the reasons why poetry and religion is declining. Reading prose should be different from reading poetry. It could be described as maybe sacred and a ritual. The poet is a shaman among his/her acolytes and can give rhythmic wisdom and it gives an echo of a wider dimension – 'as above so below'. There is not much 'vatic' content in recent verse, as is evident in Hughes and Larkin, and of course in Eliot and Yeats.

- We all need to enjoy a poem about what is in it. To create a poem needs energy and within it is a compressed message of what it is struggling to say. Accessibility is vital to link poem and poet and reader. The poem has to live free and be delightful, like a kite in the wind, but you need to know the string is there – and maybe a small kite-flier on a distant hill.

- For the above reason poem readers would like to know more of the poet: where he/she is born, education, politics, sexuality etc. The content matter of my poems are triggered from an idea – about people old age, God, food. Politics, golf, advertising, and the locked treasures in words. My immediate readers might reflect my characteristics and my interests (South-East England, Oxbridge, born pre-1939). Maybe my poems may ripple beyond.

- So far, I believe, we in the 21st Century don't have an audience for a 'serious' poet. That necessitates a number of readers – a critical mass (not how many), an integrated response to float a movement or an individual poet. There are two 'important' poets since the 1960s in the UK: Larkin and Hughes (The USA and maybe Australia has a different poetic language), though, of course, there have been 'good' poets since 1970 and now abound in tiny pools of their enthusiasts.

- Accessibility is key to find the critical mass of readers. If they find granite and forbidding verse that has no doors and windows they will walk away. Gregory Hill is sniffy about accessibility and risks it downgrading what he wants to say.

- Poetry now needs an independent trusted critic. Most of the reviews are from poets and we maybe guess they are scratching other backs and sub-texting their own slim volume and selling to their mates.

- I work on a loose iambic metre, counting syllables combined with ear and an attempt to talk a person-to-person tone of voice and hoping the reader will be urged by the rhythm and to what I'm saying. I am aware of spondees and iambics and dactyls and anapaests but if you put an 'as' or 'for' in a line the ear discounts the stress. 'Ti ti tum' and tum titi (or three of them) give a flavour to a poem like a herb in a dish. The tone of voice of my poetry seeks to be conversational, and avoid diction.

- This is about my thoughts on my current poetry. I put my tiny drop into the sea of the poetry. As each poet looks around for readers, I hope I will find an audience – be it a village pond, a stream, a river, an ocean – and anyone who likes my verse.

Go kite, carry my words sky high.
And you, reader, are the wind's whim
That jerks it up its airy climb
So it can dance and soar and fly.